Poll Tax:
The Fiscal Fake

CHATTO
CounterBlasts

Douglas
DUNN

Douglas Dunn (signature)

Poll Tax:
The Fiscal Fake

Chatto & Windus
LONDON

Published in 1990 by
Chatto & Windus Ltd
20 Vauxhall Bridge Road
London SW1V 2SA

A CIP catalogue record for this book
is available from the British Library

ISBN 0 7011 3633 2

Photoset in Linotron Ehrhardt by
Rowland Phototypesetting Ltd
Bury St Edmunds, Suffolk
Printed in Great Britain by
St Edmundsbury Press Ltd
Bury St Edmunds, Suffolk

At any normal time the ruling class will rob, mismanage, sabotage, lead us into the muck; but let popular opinion really make itself heard, let them get a tug from below that they cannot avoid feeling, and it is difficult for them not to respond.

George Orwell, *The Lion and the Unicorn*

... Men who set their minds on main matters, and sufficiently urge them, in these most difficult times, I find not many.

Milton, *The Ready and Easy Way to Establish a Free Commonwealth*

IN ENGLAND and Wales no one could have stood in very much doubt that the rates were due for reform. Hardly anyone interpreted this necessity as leading to the extinction of the rates, never mind the introduction of a poll tax. Now that domestic rates have gone, and in due course a uniform business rate, set by the central Government, will be phased in to replace non-domestic rates, the old system can look as if it enjoyed a cranky, indigenous charm. For a start, it succeeded in being a tax without being called one. Over the years it was difficult to escape from the impression that the rates were paid by millions on whom it never really registered that rates were a property or any other kind of tax. However, it would be too much to claim that the rates were taken for granted. Citizens' Advice Bureaux and local authorities themselves could point to cases of hardship, to the absolute necessity for rebates and relief, that is, for safety measures to protect the poorly off. Yet it was a system that took the ability to pay into account, while it could be argued that at the other end of prosperity a property tax, in conjunction with national income tax, proposed a more accurate assessment of taxable wealth, and a fairer levy.

For most of us, tax means income tax, VAT and, if you drive a car, road tax. Being local, the rates were somehow outside the national tax system. Most services that concern most people are administered locally – schools, social services, housing, police, the fire service, refuse collections and environmental health, street lighting, libraries, museums and art galleries, road repairs, leisure and recreation facilities, public parks, licensing, and so on. You knew what you were paying for; or, rather, you thought you were paying for these services through the rates. You were, of course, but only up to a point. Domestic rates, like the poll tax, or community charge, raised a relatively minor share of the total required. By far the largest contributor to local treasuries was, and remains, the Government itself through rate support grants, now called revenue support grants. We all pay for local government, but not in taxes paid to local authorities. National taxation is the origin of most of a local authority's finance. The Government then distributes grants in keeping with its overall financial strategy; but when much of what a local authority does is concerned with housing, welfare, social services and free-access institutions such as libraries, museums and art galleries, it soon becomes apparent that grants are vulnerable to ideology.

Why and how did the so-called community charge, the poll tax, come about? Everyone knows that the answers are to be found in pressures from within the Conservative Party. The New Conservatism is intolerant of local government. Extremists of free enterprise and market forces consider that large areas of the country are being run by councils whose philosophies and policies are not only opposed to the Government's own, but calculated to antagonise them. They see what look suspiciously like local bastions in which a belief in the Welfare State is refusing to lie down and die. For all their pious claptrap about 'local democracy', New Conservatives approve of local councils only where they control them; and so, under a banner of reform, tricked out with such concepts as 'accountability' and 'local democracy', they play a legislative game in an attempt to bring local authorities into line. The worst tendencies of old-time municipal socialism pale into insignificance when seen against this Government's ideological zeal. It is a state of mind convinced that anything that modifies the play of market forces is abhorrent. That is what the Welfare State achieved. It is what Government policy is dedicated to undo, and it has gone a large way towards asserting its will. Reform of local government finance, and the poll tax, are part of the same strategy.

Local government finance is a highly technical subject. A few weeks in its company leaves an impression of agglomerated arithmetic and few if any answers. Faced with the proposal that it needed to be redesigned, it is tempting to say, 'Yes, simplify it.' Conservative enthusiasts might even believe that this is what the Government has tried to pull off. Admittedly, it could feel like a splendid simplification were you to be paying out less than you did under the rates. But the mind that thinks in that way leaves itself open to a charge of social irresponsibility, should it be aware also that the poor are paying more than they used to, and that those whose incomes are about equal to their needs are paying the same as millionaires.

It was reported as long ago as 1976 by Layfield's Committee of Inquiry into local government finance that the professional bodies concerned with rating and valuation believed that the nature of the market did not provide enough information to permit a revaluation on the basis of rental values, on which assessments in England and Wales were made. Controlled rents, a social necessity in both public and private sectors, cramped the method of valuation to a point where it became unworkable. In a country where, at least until very recently, a three-bedroomed house in Surrey was worth much the same as a castle in Scotland, and where a two-bedroomed conversion in Gateshead might fetch the same as a cupboard in Knightsbridge, a uniform system based on property values probably looked like an embarrassment by the 1980s. It would have highlighted rich and poor, overpaid and underpaid, North and South.

Rates in Scotland were assessed on a different basis – type of dwelling, size, state of repair, amenities, garden, garage, greenhouse, even the view – and it was pronounced workable in 1983. It had been sound enough to permit a revaluation north of the border in 1978, and in 1985 when there was another revaluation it was discovered to be all too sound. The Scottish Office emerged from the experience thoroughly chastened. The last revaluation in England and Wales was as far back as 1973. Without wanting to labour the point unduly – this, after all, is a general mess, as well as, by its nature, a lot of local ones – Scotland has been made to suffer, not once, not twice, but three times. On the second occasion, with new rates bills in the April of 1986, the Scottish system was seen to be an adequate, progressive property tax. It impinged on the pockets of the government's Scottish supporters. Increases, sometimes as large as half as much again, resulted from that last round of revaluation. Around 100,000 households witnessed rises in their bills of at least a third. A larger proportion of the sum raised by the rates was shifted from the non-domestic to the domestic rates. Convinced that people vote with their pockets, the Government was prompt to lay the blame for electoral failure on these increases. An upwards trend in local rates was perceived as having momentous electoral consequences in national politics. The Government was anxious to mollify the position in Scotland, and to head off an anticipated punishment in its English constituencies. In the House of Commons on 17 December 1987, Donald Dewar, the shadow Scottish Secretary, sounded as if in little doubt that the Local Government Finance Act (which applies to England and Wales) had its origin in Scottish affairs just as much as the Abolition of Domestic Rates Etc (Scotland) Act that had been made law earlier that year.

> . . . revaluation occurred in my country. There was a revolt by the Scottish bourgeoisie and the whiff of grapeshot was seen in the streets of Eastwood and Newton Mearns.* There was a convulsive spasm in the Scottish Office and it threw up – if

* Two of the tastier suburbs in the Glasgow area.

that is the right elegant term – the poll tax. That it happened is beyond dispute. Why it happened remains something of a mystery.

In Tory circles the clamour for something to replace the rates increased in pitch and urgency. Constituency- and councillor-activists had the political gumption to realise that steps had to be taken, and quickly. A Green Paper, *Alternatives to Domestic Rates*, had already been presented in December 1981, and offered a springboard if nothing else. Written and researched under Michael Heseltine's period as Minister for the Environment, the 1981 Green Paper turned out to be less influential than a new mood in the Government itself, one of enhanced ideological daring. It was a climate in which Ministers were opened to the ideas put around by the boffins of the New Conservatism, as represented in this case by the Adam Smith Institute and, in particular, Douglas Mason's *Revising the Rating System* (1985). Mr Dewar might think that the origins of the poll tax are 'something of a mystery'; but to continue to believe in the beginnings of this fraudulent fiscal device as occult, or the result of a 'compulsive spasm', is to play down the extent to which the Government's ideological reasoning was becoming clearer to itself, nourishing its sense of purpose. Hindered by lack of numbers,

7

there was probably very little that the opposition parties could do. Where, though, were *their* alternatives?

Mr Heseltine's Green Paper did not reject out of hand the possibility of a poll tax. Between the lines, though, it is possible to detect that those working on his behalf suspected that a flat-rate poll tax across the board could be interpreted as a bit on the draconian side were it to be considered as a sole replacement for domestic rates. They suggested that its effects would depend on how much of the revenue then produced by domestic rates was to be raised by a poll tax. Out of duty to the Government's proclaimed devotion to the idea of 'accountability', they indicated that a poll tax would be 'highly perceptible'. Subsequent toilers in the vineyard of recent fiscal innovation should have taken that as a warning; but it is doubtful if they care. 'Highly perceptible, even more so than domestic rates,' it was said in the 1981 Green Paper. It is hard to miss what was, and is, meant by 'highly perceptible'. It means that a poll tax has the ability to rub the citizen's nose in the cost of things, and encourage them to vote with their pockets. 'This should strengthen the accountability of authorities to their electorates,' it says. But accounting to the national electorate has failed to deter the Government. After all, a minority of the population want a poll tax, but all of us have got it. When it comes to local government finance, however, what the Government wants to hear are these same electorates yelling, 'Too much! Too much!' That is the Government's hope. Its reform of local government finance is calculated to make it happen. The inevitably adversarial nature of democratic politics is being challenged. Evangelical impatience to domesticate voters and bring them into line with the Government's vision of society has led to the idea of accountability as something more than an excuse. In encouraging local electorates to vote against council expenditure, the legislation contains a built-in attempt to win the consent of the taxed. The Government hopes that its convictions will become the status quo of more than its customary supporters. Through the issues raised by local government it is trying to enlist converts to its philosophy as a whole. Poll tax as the financial trigger to enforce local councils to be more accountable is much the same as legislating a design on your vote, to an extent that is extraordinary in that it lies outside the usual purposes of legislation. It transgresses the spirit of our democracy.

No doubt the Government believes that its most recent move in this area of public life will prove decisive. But will it? They have been pursuing their objectives in local government since Mrs

Thatcher first took office. When Dr John Cunningham spoke as Labour's shadow Environment Minister on 16 December 1987, he pointed to 46 local government Acts in eight years, amounting to 2,730 pages of legislation and 12 major changes in local government finance. Mrs Thatcher refers to the Local Government Finance Act as 'the flagship of the Government', and she means it. Her warlike metaphor suggests that she was fed up with a flotilla of 46 little gunboats. The Local Government Finance Act might be a 'flagship', but it looks more like a task force. It has set sail against a majority of the people of Britain.

Poll taxes or capitation taxes have existed for millennia. Like most taxes it is possible to gather them only in times of relative stability backed up by a developed bureaucracy capable of compiling a census and with other information at its disposal. Money is another obvious requirement, as well as a form of governmental authority for whom taxes-in-kind no longer foot the bill for such enterprises as public works, foreign policy and extensions to the imperial banqueting suites. Poll tax was collected in Ptolemaic Egypt. 'The complete lack of receipts for this tax before the reign of Augustus,' writes a disappointed dissertationist of 1938, 'has been most disturbing.' Personally, I'm less bothered, and you might be, too; but as poll tax had its precedents before then, we can point to it as very old. Clio's eyebrows can be imagined rising in embarrassment as she watches a poll tax return to a nation famished for decency, and for whose citizens the new, fair, and satisfactory innovations of government seem as elusive as ever.

Historically, poll tax looks like the sequel to taxes-in-kind, heavily armed border-crossing, plunder, confiscation and Thy Neighbour's Ox, but it has persisted. Its principle has proved highly attractive – everyone pays. In the days when the remoter regions of most countries were celebrated for their truculent tribes, gathering any kind of tax was a military operation. Nowadays computerised registers of who and where you are might in some quarters make it seem the easiest form of tax to levy and collect, in spite of the hazards that statistical controls introduce to the field of civil rights and the justifiable privacy of the citizen. All you do is post the bills and wait for the receipts, while, in the meantime, you work out rebates and try to keep your register up-to-the-minute.

When Charles I raised a poll tax in 1641 it was graduated according to ability to pay. For example, a duke was charged £100 and an esquire £10. Those not rated specifically were assessed locally according to circumstances. It was an emergency tax demanded by the need to pay off the army as quickly as possible; and there is something of an emergency feel about the present poll tax, which has been got together in a hurry to appease a minority of discontented voters as well as to satisfy the ideological appetite of self-confident New Conservatism. It is an important sally in the general assault on the sort of society that New Conservatives believe they must dismantle before remaking it in the image of their inverted Utopia. It is of a piece with privatisation, which would not make sense without the Government's resentful intervention in local government finance. It coincides with designs on the NHS, politically motivated meddling with education at all levels except the private, student loans, and with 'reforms' that are calculated to undermine the benefits of the Welfare State to the poor and disadvantaged.

It is not that a poll tax is a throwback to earlier days when capitalism was allowed to produce both profit and misery. A poll tax was seen as anachronistic long before the word capitalism was coined in 1854. What else can you say of a form of tax first raised in England in the reign of Edward III, with a boosted version imposed by his grandson, Richard II, a tax which formed the major cause of Wat Tyler's rebellion, and that was finally abolished in this country in the reign of William III? What else can you say of a tax that is perhaps best known from Tsarist Russia, where it was known as the 'soul tax'? Or a form of tax imposed in the Turkish provinces of Europe, where, as a capitation tax, it was meant to be taken literally – pay up or lose your head? If it is a tax that indicates more-or-less civilised procedures – more civilised than official brigandage, if nothing else – it also indicates a stage of development which our society is supposed to have surpassed centuries ago. To illustrate this it needs only a mention of how British colonial administrations in Africa used a poll tax to try to bring traditional populations into a money economy. Incredible as it might seem, a similar colonial psychology is threaded through the present poll tax. This time the 'natives' are all in the 'mother country', which might even explain why Scotland was used as a laboratory for such an extraordinary anachronism.

J. R. McCulloch, a nineteenth-century economist, described poll tax as a tax on wages when paid to a government. For those who are less than wealthy, the present poll tax or so-called community charge is a tax on income whether or not that is how the Government defines it. How could it be anything else? It is not an income tax, but a tax of so much a head; it is a poll tax pretending to be a 'community charge' set as payment for the services provided by local councils. Or so the Government does not say; it says it *is* a 'community charge'. But any tax operates in relation to a citizen's ability to pay it. That is very emphatically the case in a country like Britain where many people are poorly paid for what they do; and when they are unemployed or for other reasons obliged to be the dependants of various social services, they are supported inadequately.

The confusion of poll tax with 'community charge' is perhaps little more than an example of Government-speak. Opponents of the tax will call it by one name, its supporters by another. Whatever you call it, its existence is likely to raise arguments that look similar to those that were rehearsed endlessly about the inequitable nature of the rates. This time the difference is likely to be that those on average earnings or slightly above will be carrying much more of the burden than the better-off. Nor is it impossible that the better-off will complain that they are *still* paying more than they should. They could claim that as 'private sector people' they use local government services less than those with average or slightly above average incomes. As it happens, I witnessed political pressure of that kind in the American city of Akron, Ohio, in the mid-1960s. It was effective, and the municipality was obliged to cut its budget severely. The police force was reduced, as was the fire service; alternate street-lamps were switched off. In no time at all the burgled, raped, mugged and incinerated middle class of Akron was complaining vociferously that these consequences were not what they'd meant, not at all what they'd had in mind. They'd forgotten, or disregarded, just how pervasive and essential a local government's activities really are. They'd forgotten, too, that they have to be paid for. It is only a hunch of experience, but Britain's New Conservatives of the late twentieth century could find themselves learning the same lesson as their American counterparts. You could be more confident about that had American conservatism learned its lesson. Ideology, though, socialist, conservative, or whatever, is immune to instruction. That is a definition of ideology. For that matter, it comes close to a definition of government, too, and, certainly, of this present Government.

The 1981 Green Paper was disinclined to consider a poll tax beyond suggesting a small flat-rate figure – the sum mentioned was £25–£30 per annum – as a supplement to a major revenue-raising tax. In its time that would have raised between £1000 and £1200 million, or considerably less than the estimated £1800 million of profits from illicit drugs dealing now circulating through the British banking system. Mr Heseltine seems to have been prepared to accept that minor tax as a support to local sales and income taxes or a revised method of assessing rates.

Between 1982 and 1986 the Government's impatience with the local authorities had intensified, while it was becoming increasingly aware of the political consequences of revaluation in Scotland. *Paying for Local Government*, the 1986 Green Paper, is a breezier, far more determined, as well as statistically equipped document than its predecessor. It speaks only of 'adequate services'; there is no mention of excellence. It concentrates on 'paying', not on provision. Its tempo buoys its considerable length on a relish for the changes it describes. Where the earlier Green Paper stated that a common criticism of the rates was that they were 'unfairly shared as between different types of household or as between people occupying property of a similar kind in different local authority areas', by 1986 the terms employed were much blunter. 'The burden of rates is carried on too few shoulders,' it declared, introducing an argument that is remarkably transparent in its deviousness and political intent. Rates as a property tax could be interpreted in that manner, but only if you felt opposed to its redistributive nature which, of course, it shared with income tax. Those who live in big houses paid more than those who live in small ones. But who other than proprietors and tenants could be identified as responsible for rates bills? 'Domestic rates are paid by a minority of local electors,' the 1986 Green Paper stated, as if expecting the reader to believe it without first asking a few questions.

'Electors' cues us to the Government's hope that the poll tax will generate electoral effects. Those 'too few shoulders', that 'minority of local electors', amounts to a politically loaded demographic overview and a slippery misuse of figures. It also jettisons the politically neutral, sweetly British term 'householders'.

> There are over 35 million electors in England. Of these about 18 million are liable to pay rates. Of course, many of those remaining will be spouses of ratepayers; but they are not billed direct, nor do they personally make any payment to their local authority; and other adult members of ratepayers' families may have even less appreciation of the cost of local services.

What the passage does not reveal is that, of the 19.5 million people in Britain who received a rates bill, some 12 million of them had spouses; and to say that wives and husbands of ratepayers were not 'billed direct' shows a curious remoteness from the normal workings of family finance. 31.5 million

17

people, then, contributed to the rates. Husbands and wives, adult children living at home, grandparents and other dependent relatives, are now billed for the poll tax, through what amounts to an expensive drive to publicise the cost of local services and promote a squeeze on local authority spending by means of an anticipated change in how citizens will vote. As well as reforming local finance, the Act seeks to reform local electors.

When compared with the actual figures and with the realities of family budgeting, the Government's talk of 'too few shoulders' and a 'minority of electors' looks dangerously close to political fraudulence. Other figures in the 1986 Green Paper give some idea of the issues that its authors were prepared to evade. Of that 18 million ratepayers in England, about 12 million paid in full. 3 million received rebates, and another 3 million full relief. Half the electorates of Wales and Scotland were eligible to pay rates. 15 per cent in Wales and 21 per cent in Scotland received rebates, while those who received full relief in Wales amounted to 18 per cent, and in Scotland 17 per cent. Something like indignation is detectable behind the Government's statement that 'Those who receive full relief can vote for higher services without having to pay anything towards them.' But while that complaint provoked cries of outrage from New Conservatives, it did so only through its failure to take seriously the reasons why 3 million were rebated in part and 3 million rebated in full. Low pay, unemployment and an inadequate, breadline system of benefits explain to a large degree why rebates and relief were necessary, just as they will continue to be necessary with the poll tax, unless turning the screw on the poor is what the Government wants. At the very least the Government is prepared to risk a growth in real poverty while chasing its psychological goal of making local councils more accountable to their populations.

In its dishonest, almost laughably gruesome use of language, the Government speaks of establishing a 'financial link' between the poor and their local authorities. Even 20 per cent of the poll tax will subtract hurtfully from the incomes of those who subsist on benefits. Since 1988, after changes in the social security Acts, people in these circumstances have been paying 20 per cent of rates, and cases of real hardship were and are the result. Such a 'financial link' comes at a time when an unpublished report prepared by the Child Poverty Action Group for the European Commission revealed in December 1989 that poverty in Britain doubled between 1975 and 1985. According to the criteria used, 3.6 million people lived in poverty in 1975, 5 million in 1980 and 6.6 million in 1985. It can be assumed that the Government's innovations in social security have done little, if anything, to arrest or turn the trend of poverty in this country. Nor will the poll tax achieve anything except to make matters worse for the disadvantaged. It was disingenuous of Nicholas Ridley to whinge in the House of Commons (December 1987) that rates rebates were then running close to £1.5 billion per annum. His disgruntlement should have been directed at the *causes* of slender means. Earlier in the same speech Mr Ridley pointed out that 40 per cent of homes in England with above average rateable values were occupied by those with below average incomes. It was the kind of anomaly that a revised method of assessing valuations, or local income and sales taxes, could have ironed out.

A politically disinterested solution to the problems seems to have been discounted by the Government at an early stage between the Green Papers of 1981 and 1986. Instead, they have added to the local tax burden carried by those whose earnings are average or a bit above, worsened the position of the poor for the sake of establishing a 'financial link' (so derisory a concept that it makes you doubt the sanity of whoever invented it), and flattered the well-off. In his earlier remark Mr Ridley creates the unfortunate impression of directing a dirty look at the low-paid and the poor whose rebates cost the taxpayer an allegedly extortionate sum each year. When seen against the £20 billion of national loss incurred by privatisations so far, and written off, that £1.5 billion looks like a very small amount. Between the two figures the difference is astounding; but the New Conservatism sees that sort of discrepancy as an ideological triumph, as a measure of victory in its contest with local government and the Welfare State. It is only too willing to make us pay for the modifications it has been intent on imposing on our society. This is a serious charge when you consider Britain as a whole. Take into account, however, that Scotland, Wales and the North of England did not vote for these policies, and a clearer portrait of the Government's wilfulness begins to emerge.

Without actually saying so, what the Government opposed was a property tax, which, in general, although not always, was incomes-related, and could have been improved. What it wanted to achieve was a redistribution of the local tax burden within a national context. No Government Minister has ever come clean on the subject to the extent of explaining why, but all along the intention has been to change taxation's redistributive flow. A flat-rate poll tax echoes cuts in the higher rate of income tax. While the 1981 Green Paper failed to offer a separate discussion of a poll tax under the heading of *Fairness* (which it managed with other alternatives to the rates), it did at least suggest that 'As an entirely new tax, a poll tax would have rather different implications for the shape and structure of the total tax system.' Never mind that 'an entirely ancient tax' would have been a more accurate description. Sales tax, or local income tax, would 'overlap much more directly with existing national taxes'. By 1986 the avoidance of an overlap with redistributive or progressive principles of taxation was what the Government sought. Revision gave way to a more radical reform that abolished the rates entirely, and excluded the fairer alternative of a local incomes tax.

By 1986 the Government was exercising to the full its 'legitimate interest' in how much local authorities spend, borrow, and raise in local taxation. It is intent on taking this 'legitimate interest' as far as it can go. Exchequer grants to local government in England had already been reduced from 60 per cent of expenditure in 1980/81 to 40 per cent in 1985/86. In Wales they had dropped from 74 per cent to 67 per cent, and in Scotland from 68.5 to 57.7 per cent. In the words of the 1986 Green Paper, 'stronger measures' were necessary, measures, that is, that would go a stage further than the 1984 Rates Act by which the Government acquired the power to set limits on rates levied in England and Wales. The reason for this was clear. Cuts in exchequer grants obliged local authorities to put up domestic and non-domestic rates, and the temptation was to increase the load borne by commercial and industrial properties. Were the cutting of public expenditure to meet the Government's requirements, then legislation to peg the rates was necessary in an effort to force recalcitrant administrations to behave themselves. Simultaneously, the Government felt the need to pacify its supporters whose rates bills had been increasing as a negative, irritating rebound from the Government's own policy. The Rates Act came into force in 1985/86. In Scotland, however, the Government acquired similar powers ahead of the rest of the island, and limits were fixed in 1983. Scotland had a workable method of assessing rateable values; it was punished for it. By no stretch of the imagination would the Government examine the efficient, *Scottish* system of evaluation, and recommend it to the rest of the island.

Efficiency is not the Government's yardstick; what it is after is cheapness. In 1984/85, 16 per cent of total UK tax receipts were spent on local government. Latest figures available to the authors of the 1986 Green Paper indicated the scale of local government. It employed 3 million people, two-thirds of whom were full-time. Local government's cost amounted to a quarter of all public expenditure, or around 11 per cent of Gross Domestic Product. In a round sum, the local authorities spent about £45 billion. Just by saying so the Government meant (it still means it) that local government employed too many people and cost too much. That is, the country cost too much. The country would have to get cheaper before the Government could take it seriously and treat it with respect. The country would have to toe the line and do what it was told. Now that poll tax will be the only source of funds that local authorities can raise, squeezing will mean its steady increase until it forces either 'accountability' or governmental pegging. Local authorities will then be faced with the necessity of reducing some services and cutting others altogether. Some are likely to be privatised. Services will slip from excellent to adequate to inadequate to non-existent. Charges will start to be introduced for the use of libraries, museums and art galleries, and other facilities in which free access is at present enshrined in public principle. Once the pips start to squeak (and they will) the country will become cheaper. It might also start to become cheap and nasty. Services hived off to private companies now waiting for their opportunities will ensure that those who share the Government's philosophy will do quite nicely out of the new arrangements.

'Fairness' seems to have been banished from the thoughts of the authors of the 1986 Green Paper; or else the objection to a flat-rate poll tax that was noted in 1981 – that it would represent 'a greater proportion of a lower income than a higher one' – was given the nod as a positively attractive feature. Complaints that the old rates were inequitable now find themselves replaced by objections of a very similar kind directed at the poll tax. The difference is that the not-so-well-off are paying more than they were as well as disproportionately more than their better-off fellow citizens both in the same district and elsewhere in the country. Evidence for this state of affairs will take a little time to filter through in England and Wales; but it is already available in Scotland where the poll tax has been in operation since April 1989.

By October 1989, in its Bulletin No. 24, the Scottish Local Government Information Unit was able to reveal that there had been a major shift in the burden of paying for regional council services. (In the Scottish system of local government, there are Regions and Districts.) For example, in Strathclyde Region, the District of Bearsden and Milngavie accounted for 1.8 per cent of poll tax income for 1989/90, while it had contributed 2.8

per cent of domestic rates income the year before. The saving for each adult is £127.22. These figures reflect only the regional component of the poll tax. Even so, they expose the social bias of the tax. Eastwood District now contributes 35.9 per cent less than it did in rates, a saving of £121.18 per adult. Wealthier parts of Scotland tend to reflect decreases or small increases, with rural areas showing quite considerable increases per adult. In Fife Region, where there are three Districts, Dunfermline and Kirkcaldy, which are more industrial, contribute more in poll tax than they did in rates. North-East Fife, by and large prosperous, contributes 13.2 per cent less than previously, a modest saving of £4.87 for each adult. As the Scottish Local Government Information Unit claims, it would be possible to compile an analysis of losses and gains ward by ward and street by street. More precise research might be necessary in order to be convincing, but what it will illustrate is that areas that were of high rateable value in the past will be seen to benefit at the expense of areas that were formerly of low rateable value. For the well-off, the modest redistribution of the tax burden that is involved seems hardly worth the consequences likely to be endured by citizens with lower incomes. On the whole the pattern will be gains for the wealthy, losses for families and individuals with average to slightly above average incomes, and losses for the poorly off. Can anyone really believe that this is a coincidental feature of the poll tax?

The so-called community charge can look like ideological self-indulgence, while the reform of local government finance of which it is part is dedicated clearly to bringing about wholesale cuts in public expenditure at the expense of local public services. Considered in terms of people and what they must pay, the further down the social scale you look, the more severe its practical effects will be seen to be. That is the conclusion already drawn by the experience of the poll tax in Scotland. Even with 'safety nets', the purpose of which is to keep revenue from non-domestic rates and exchequer grants at the same level for four years in England and Wales, and from three to five years in Scotland, the shift in the tax burden has become obvious. Once 'safety nets' have been removed and the poll tax left free to operate unhindered by concession, cross-financing and restraint, then the obviousness of the Government's intentions will begin to bite.

During the latest Conservative Party Conference it was announced that steps would be taken to ensure that no one was more than £3 a week worse off under the poll tax. While the gesture was welcomed, it soon became obvious in Scotland (where people were looking for some money back, and not unreasonably) that its application created an administrative headache of the first magnitude. Not long after the announcement was made, finance officers in the Scottish local authorities were entertaining grave doubts over the possibility of relief being calculated by the end of 1989 for those the concession was meant to benefit, including pensioners, the disabled, and others who were exempted from rates. The problems were technical and related to the awkwardness of matching lists with lists without having to revert to old-fashioned clerical work on an epic scale. The need for relief was accepted, and the political will existed to attempt to put it into effect.

By 10 November, Ray Michie, the Liberal Democrat MP for Argyll and Bute, was claiming that the poll tax had gone 'from an unmitigated disaster to an unparalleled shambles'. Mrs Michie drew attention to the administrative nightmare caused by the Government's sudden changes in the rules produced by growing anxiety at the possible effects of the poll tax in England and Wales. Through newspaper reports and articles more and more people in Scotland were becoming aware of the poll tax and its implications. In the *Glasgow Herald*'s report on Mrs Michie's parliamentary questions, for example, it was remarked that Strathclyde Region was then handling around 2000 changes a day to the poll tax register, and over 44,000 a month. As for pensioners and the disabled in Scotland, who did not pay rates, their entitlement to relief is limited to what they pay above £156 a year under the poll tax. From zero rates to £156 a year is rather a lot for the ordinary pensioner. There is also the controversy of whether the Scottish Office will link the poll tax transitional relief scheme to its notional figures or to the figures actually levied by each authority.

Hardly a day has gone by in the Scottish press without some piece of news about the poll tax. It will be the same in England. Popular dissent inclines towards belatedness. To men and women now in their forties and early fifties it feels as if we are living in a different time than the one our fathers promised. It is bewildering that we should find ourselves living through such a moment. A subtle, ideologically determined anachronism is being imposed on the population and backed up by the latest gadgetry. In Scotland alone the poll tax's hardware is estimated to have cost around £30 million. Why were the New Conservatism and its policies allowed to triumph? Part of the answer lies in the Prime Minister's personality and presence, which many voters in some areas of England actually seem to like. A major factor must be the staleness that the Labour Party allowed itself to slip into when it was in power, generating compromise and a lack of clarity. Reasons for which the entire Labour Party cannot be blamed made it seem no longer worthy of public trust. There being but a single viable alternative, the New Conservatism got in; and this stunt of half-mindedness and self-interest having been performed three times, it is impossible to be optimistic about a fourth opportunity.

When it becomes better known in England and Wales, the poll tax might turn out to be the catalyst that has been lacking so far and that will make the Government accountable to public opinion. Admittedly, there are additional factors at work in Scotland, where a resurgent national identity has begun to make itself felt in politics and culture, and where conscience was never felt as 'the beggar's virtue'. In Scotland, this present Government is seen as being of the Government, by the Government, and for the Government. It certainly isn't of, by and for the people of Scotland. From north of the border England once again looks the way George Orwell described it, 'a land of snobbery and privilege, ruled largely by the old and silly'. No, England is not like that; it just looks like it. But the New Conservatism grows older day by day; and it has always maintained links with a much older Conservatism altogether. It is Yeoman and Merchant Conservatism in electronic disguise.

Poll tax can be justified only by the Government to itself within its narrow, obsessive scripture of principles, its intellectual fictions. Freedom, for instance, would appear to have been redefined as the freedom to buy and sell. A philosophical hierarchy has been tampered with for the sake of practical politics and economic elbow-room. The greatest freedom is believed to be that enjoyed by the man or woman who exercises commercial or industrial wealth-making initiative. People with that sort of talent are extremely important to a society that does not desire and has never been forced to suffer the State's control of legitimate private enterprise. Yet their present adoration distracts alarmingly from the political status of freedom in a democratic society. It directs a degree of contempt towards the freedom of citizens whose talents might lie in other activities, or whose potential remains unknown, because it was never given a chance, or assumed to be a possibility in the first place.

Between the publication of the second Green Paper and 31 August 1986, when the period for consultation ended, local authorities and many others had criticised its proposals on all the grounds put forward by the Government to prove the soundness of 'the most radical reform of local government finance this century'. The new system was condemned as technically inadequate, unfair, and

unlikely to encourage local democratic 'accountability'. By implication, something very wrong in-
deed had been going on for years in the nation's
Town Halls, and it was high time that the causes
of this financial evil were led away and drowned by
the Pied Pipers of the New Conservatism.

Cuts in public expenditure are what the Government has been after all along, and it has been
prepared to mislead the country in order to achieve
them. Fanatical free enterprisers like to give the
impression that local government spending has
been reckless, unprincipled, lavish and uncon-
trolled. They do not like to mention that in 1978/
79 local government expenditure amounted to 10.5
per cent of Gross Domestic Product, and that by
1986/87 it accounted for 10.7 per cent. The difference of 0.2 per cent does not look like an upsurge
of spending about which a Government should
get hot and bothered. Why, then, such wholesale
reforms, extending to a controversial and anti-
quarian poll tax? The only answer that seems to
make sense is that the Government's legitimate
interest in the reasonable control of local government expenditure goes further than its public
avowals. Local authorities know this, and most of
them resent it; they know that much of what they
do slots into the Government's tedious definition
of the public sector as a negative, unprofitable

32

hindrance to private enterprise. Most of them realise that their initiatives are vulnerable before the Government's obdurate mentality. They know that the purpose of the new legislation is to impair, or subvert, the ability of local councils to sustain their services at their existing quality. The poll tax and other changes in local government finance are not intended to improve services, nor are they directed at local councils in a spirit of administrative benevolence. Nor are they intended as benign in how they affect a majority of ordinary citizens, or that large minority who are described accurately as living in poverty. Like 'freedom', the Public Good, or Common Weal, has been redefined. 'Public' and 'common' have become terms of abuse, while 'good' and 'weal' apply only to the Government and its supporters. A 'radical reform'? You can say that again. The poll tax is not just a devious fake; it is a form of pollution, issued, ironically enough, from the office of the Minister for the Environment.

Local authorities are being used to bring to the public's attention an awareness of how much they cost. That is, the public is being encouraged to vote for cheaper services and less of them. Through the uniform business rate, the Government has removed the largest source of variable tax from the control of the councils, while Government grants are determined by control, not need. In 1988/89, for example, 51.1 per cent of the expenditure of the Central Region in Scotland was raised from domestic and non-domestic rates. Now only 19.7 per cent is raised by the poll tax, leaving the remainder to be provided by a Government that distrusts what local authorities do. Spending over the Government's idea of *ought* (and it can be turned into a *must* through capping) will have to be met through increases in the poll tax. Strathclyde Region has already suggested that the tax for 1990/91 will be 15 per cent more than this year. Because both major sources of funds are likely to be recalcitrant, especially after the end of 'safety nets', and once the Government feels that the new system is established, the 'gearing effect' will become more visible. An increase in spending of around 5 per cent will lead to a rise in the poll tax of about 20 per cent.

At the moment, these figures look like make-believe arithmetic; but they will become real. England and Wales have registered for the so-called community charge (at great expense, probably in the region of £300 million), but no one there knows exactly what their bill will be. If the Scottish experience is anything to go by, then in a great many cases bills will be bigger than the figures announced by the Government on 6 November 1989. On the whole, though, what these figures demonstrate is that the poll tax 'targets' councils run by opposition parties (even with 'safety nets' and at the expense of cheaper, perhaps Tory councils). They show, too, who gains, and who loses, when seen in terms of people, prosperity and deprivation, rather than the hostility between Government and the councils. In the City of London the average rates bill per adult, plus 4 per cent for inflation, was £823 in 1989/90. The Government computes the long-run community charge without 'safety net' as £362, and with the 'safety net', £356. In Brent, these three figures came out as £495 for the old rates, £463 poll tax without 'safety net' and £480 with. In North Tyneside, where average rates were £317, the poll tax with 'safety net' comes out at £342. In that particular case, you can work out the increase for yourself, and think of a family, perhaps a couple with two children still under eighteen, whose earnings are not far above the national average. Eighteenth birthdays are likely to become ambivalent celebrations – the 'key of the door' (as it used to be called) plus a community charge registration form. For those indifferent to politics (and it has been estimated that this is a significant minority of young people) there will be an incentive to dodge tax registration *and* the electoral register *and* trace-leaving where data can be reported to officials. Democracy is not encouraged by the

35

poll tax; it is discouraged by it. Between citizens, local government, and central Government, the relationship has been changed for the worse.

But will these figures really be what the English local authorities levy? The shadow Environment Secretary, Bryan Gould, described the proposed average poll tax figure of £278 as a 'hopeless mirage'. The Association of County Councils (which is controlled by the Conservatives) declared itself disappointed by the figures, saying that it would allow for an increase in expenditure of only 3.8 per cent. Again, what happened in Scotland might indicate the uncertainty in which the Government's figures should be held. Of 53 Scottish district councils, reflecting the combined regional and district poll tax figure, 46 charged more than the Scottish Office's estimate, six charged less, and one matched it. Several councils charging more did so by slight amounts, but in most cases the discrepancy is considerable. Aberdeen is a striking example. Estimated at £201, the poll tax sum that was actually billed came to £304. East Lothian's inhabitants were for a time led to believe that they would pay £307, and discovered that the local council wanted £374. In Edinburgh, where taxpayers in Scotland's capital expected to pay £313, they had to meet bills for £392. You could say that 'accountability' has been operating from day one of the poll tax in Scotland; but if the population has failed to rally round its local councils, it seems fair to interpret the national mood as one in which responsibility for the poll tax's introduction, size and likely increases is laid firmly before the Government. Hostility will intensify as the Government's figures for other parts of the island become better known – Kent, Buckinghamshire, Norfolk, Lincolnshire, Devon, Dorset, and so on. Its policies having widened political and social differences in the country, the Government now seems more than willing to prise them open through a local tax that favours its natural supporters and offends everyone else.

All of which is in perfect keeping with the regressive nature of any flat-rate poll tax. Amotz Morag, in his book *On Taxes and Inflation* (1965), refers to poll tax as unacceptable to society. Adam Smith, whose name is appealed to so often by right-wing philosophers of money, believed that sums raised by a poll tax tied to incomes 'might always have been found in some other way much more convenient to the people'. Smith's advice percolated through to every modern economist, it would seem, with the significant exceptions of those fashionable in Downing Street and in the Scottish Office. Morag writes that

37

if distributional effects of taxation could be disregarded, the poll tax would be ideal, for, if the possibilities of suicide, emigration, and a deliberate decrease in birth rates are excluded, it has no allocational effects.

The 'inconvenience' of the poll tax arises from the form which the visionary archaeologists who devised it intended that it should take – a flat-rate charge of so-much a head within a local authority's area, exempting only children and the dead ('coterminous with the electoral roll' was the phrase). To that can be added annual running costs – the poll tax is twice as expensive administratively. And it cost a lot to set up. Also to be taken into account is the loss of the rates, a tax that was widely understood, and that was nothing like as inert or incorrigible to reform as the Government chose to make out.

For look what has happened! Having noticed late in the day that a tax that is not founded *in principle* on ability to pay is intrinsically unfair, the Government has had to bend over backwards to persuade us that this unfair impost can be made to work as fairly as if equity had been its intention all along. At least temporarily, the Government has had to take into account unpalatable aspects of the country such as poverty, low incomes, the predicaments of pensioners and the disabled, as well as economic differences between one part of the island and another.

Whether the Government's concessions will be permanent is quite another matter, as is how important they might be to the legislation they have devised as an effective means of curbing local government expenditure. It can look as if the Government has stood itself on its head, or driven its 'flagship' into drydock for a rest before a refit. What the rebates and concessions mean is that not a lot less than half of the 35 million proposed poll-tax payers will be entitled to reductions to some extent. By the time you figure out how many people will be paying the so-called community charge in full, the figure looks suspiciously close to the number who paid rates. If nothing else, it shows how close to a 'progressive' tax the old rates really were within a picture of the country's taxable wealth as represented by property or households. All this fuss about nothing? you may well ask. But no, the poll tax has not been made into a 'progressive' tax related to ability to pay; it has simply been trimmed by concessionary measures and by 'safety nets', and it is to be doubted if there is anything permanent about either. That the Government has placed itself in an unholy mess is undeniable; but this Government is as nimble as the witch's cat – it will try to right itself ideologically and in practice, and it will try to steer its flagship back on course. To remember all those Acts concerning local government that preceded this one is to realise that the Government is a very long way from being finished with the subject.

The sheer indelicacy of mind and feeling, the crude cunning with which manipulative legislation has been framed in the pretence of serving democratic accountability, as well as its last-minute concessions, point to the fraudulence of the Government's would-be reforms. At no time have its spokesmen admitted that the partiality of the poll tax is what it likes about it. As a regressive tax, simply by being on the statute books, it unbalances the national system of taxation. It sits among the nation's laws like an archaic threat, a statutory gargoyle that growls at the idea of local government as much as its allegedly over-expensive activities. Inroads have already been made on progressive taxation through cuts in the higher rate of income tax, for which a decrease in the basic rate was inadequate compensation for the progressive system as a whole. Considered or casual attempts have been made to force taxation to fulfil the ideological requirements of the Government instead of the socially equitable objective of spreading the tax burden, which would serve the country.

Progressive taxation is natural to a country like

Britain where extremes of wealth and poverty can be seen every day of the week. Its 'natural' balance, however, seems never to have been struck. The Labour Party tends to exaggerate it in one direction, and the Conservative Party in another, while the New Conservatism caricatures it altogether. It leaves you with the feeling that progressive taxation is just one more of those national facts of which the New Conservatism disapproves. It is only fair to mention that there seems to be opposition within the Government's own Party to this tendency to flatter higher incomes and treat lower incomes with a psychological contempt that is greedy in practice. High interest rates – and the interest rate is used as a kind of tax – hit hard on those with average and slightly above average incomes. (Those hit even harder are the recently unemployed, even if for only a relatively short period.)

Such issues have to enter the picture, as must low levels in benefits and changes in the social security laws in which 'targeting' often means robbing the poor to support the very poor. Michael Mates's amendment during the second reading of the Local Government Finance Act attempted to tie the scale of payments for the so-called community charge to levels of income tax. It could hardly be said to go far enough – for instance, those earning insufficient to pay income tax at all would have been charged half the poll-tax levy in their local authority areas. If nothing else, though, it tried to introduce the idea of a graduated scale, and it enlisted a good deal of support. Even with concessions and rebates, a graduated scale does not exist. Instead, a flat-rate poll tax is nibbled at by regulations that can be changed without amending the Act. Both the Abolition of Domestic Rates Etc (Scotland) Act and the Local Government Finance Act are still there. They are in force. So, too, are what they stand for. They represent a virtually complete control of local government finance, and, therefore, of local government itself, by central Government. They represent a uniform business rate, replacing non-domestic rates, of which the CBI and other organisations are at best suspicious, but which they seem to distrust as more ominous than they have yet declared. They also represent, and enforce, a flat-rate poll tax already beaten into shape by public opinion, or the Government's fear of it, to look like a progressive tax. But it is not a progressive tax. It is a flat-rate tax that has buckled under the pressure of the country's disadvantaged citizens, who have not, as yet, spoken for themselves so much as been spoken up for by their Members of Parliament – of all parties – who have a better sense of how people feel than the Government itself.

The case for a thoroughly progressive system of

taxation was put by an American writer on the
subject as far back as 1938. In an agreeably elegant
passage on an inelegant subject, he wrote that it
rests on

> the case against inequality – on the ethical or
> aesthetic judgement that the prevailing distribution
> of wealth reveals a degree (and/or kind) of in-
> equality which is distinctly evil or unlovely.*

When legislation expresses negative judgements of
that type, then a fair measure is gained of how far
a Government is prepared to go beyond a tacit
acceptance of inequality. Encouragement is being
given to the worsening of social divisions within the
country, and that is a serious accusation. Issues
concerned with the poll tax will tend to bring the
Government's psychology into the open. It already
seems clear enough that there are kinds of people by
whom the Government is affronted or embarrassed,
and that there are areas of the country that it
distrusts and dislikes. When its assault on local
government began in 1980 some of it was explained
by a disgracefully positive reaction to racial prejudice or prejudice against other minorities, particu-

---

* Henry C. Simons, *Personal Income Taxation*, University of
Chicago Press, 1938.

larly in London and other English cities. Black and Asian households often tend to contain a large number of adults or extended families above the age of eighteen, and the same can be said of many working-class or agricultural families throughout Britain. The effects of the poll tax on such households could be extremely serious.

In Scotland we have now reached the point where over 100,000 people have been issued with summary warrants (approved by a sheriff's court, after application by a local council, and sent out by sheriffs' officers), while others, including the Region where I live (Fife) have received from sheriffs' officers a notice to the effect that they must now proceed with the next debt-collecting stage, which is Poinding (pronounced 'pinding'; it means a warrant sale of goods equal in assessment to a debt) and/or Arrestment. Comparable terms in English law are distraint of possessions, and attachment of earnings or a bank account. Newspaper estimates suggest that as much as 25 per cent of the registered electorate in Glasgow have paid nothing. By December 1989, Strathclyde Region, by far the largest in Scotland in terms of population, had still to send out its summary warrants. That figure of 100,000 could easily be trebled. On one day, Lothians Region popped 76,756 summary warrants into the post. In a single day, more than 76,000

Scots were given the opportunity of backing down, paying up, or becoming outlaws. Before you can say 'Rob Roy McGregor', blokes in tartan plaids and waving basket swords will be asking you if you are for the poll tax or agin it.

Yet the choice can hardly be a simple one of paying or not paying. Men and women who have chosen to resist paying the poll tax on grounds of principle and conscience might form a smaller percentage of the total than the political activists believe. It would be convenient if self-aware protesters formed a majority, but the suspicion remains that those who have received summary warrants so far might be people too poor to pay, or too confused to know what is being asked of them. In that case, the poll tax will be seen to be an even worse tax than was previously believed, and protesters will have every right to feel themselves justified. Some 700,000 of the Scottish electorate are in part-default by three months or more. The Anti-Poll Tax Federation (with which I am not associated) estimates that between 500,000, and a million summary warrants might have to be issued by around the end of January 1990. One bureaucratic masterpiece follows another. Throughout Scotland, Citizens' Advice Bureaux are concerned that some authorities will be harsher than others; they plead for consistency. Grampian Region, for example, attempted a warrant sale on an elderly widow in MacDuff who refused to register for the tax. Protesters staged a sit-in, and it transpired that the sheriffs' officers had no authorisation to poind the widow's three-piece suite and wall unit. Alex Falconer, a Member of the European Parliament, who lives in Dunfermline, has been threatened with a warrant sale for refusing to register for a tax that he loathes. This is bad news for me. Dunfermline is in Fife, and visions of my first editions being carried off in a bailiff's bag are extremely unpleasant. Freezing the bank accounts of non-payers is disliked by the Scottish bankers; they suggest that the cost of recovering debts on that scale could cost £20 million. Arrestment of earnings has led to the fear that some employees could be sacked. No local government in Scotland favours warrant sales. However they are bound to pursue defaulters with the full process of law.

A tax that was always meant to be perceptible is being administered in Scotland by local authorities which to a very large extent are opponents of the Government. It is being done in such a way that the perceptibility of the tax has been puffed up beyond the wildest dreams of the political antiquarians who devised it. It has come to the point where opponents of the tax have called the Labour authorities the 'Tories' tallymen'. That might mean more in Scotland than it does in England, but there you are . . . I just happen to believe that it will come to mean as much in England and Wales, and I believe that it will get worse and worse.

A Scottish Private Member's Bill is to be introduced to try to ban warrant sales; but English authorities have an even worse track record in debt-collecting. You can't go to prison for debt in Scotland; you can in England. Between 1979 and 1987 no fewer than 3,869 people were sent to jail in England for debts owed for rates to local councils.

Poor People's Cafés

Not down-and-outs,
Though some come close,
Nor layabouts
Trading pathos
For tea and bread,
But simply poor
In this lowered
Epoch, its door
Stiff to their shoves,
No easy entrance
To decent groves
Of furtherance.

Steamed spectacles
As I sit down
At the wiped spills,
Raising the tone
(Or so it seems)
Against their will.
National dreams
Have gone downhill
And there's a hoax
In every mouth,
Demented jokes
And diddled truth.

Such rooms translate
Half-lies in how
Waitresses wait
On out-at-elbow
Customers by
Puddled sills, drips
From windows. Pie,
Baked beans and chips;
Tea, sausage roll . . .
That smell of coat;
Dried rain, and a scowl
From a dead thought.

Two women brood;
Their roll-ups burn –
Smoked solitude,
Both taciturn,
Each parodies
In somewhere else;
And somebody's
Companion smells
His burgered plate
Then starts to eat.
Waitresses wait
On slippered feet.

He talks to a cup;
She stirs their tea
Then holds it up,
A wedded pity
In how they share –
Her sip, his sip;
It looks like prayer,
Companionship
In a belief
In the unknown,
Elderly grief
And most hopes gone.

Down in the dumps
Indignant notes
Compile a glimpse
Of huddled coats
And this kitchen's
Primitive broth
Where tendered pence
This twentieth
Day of the dead
Winter, transact
Important bread
And stale neglect.

On these borders
Being poor
Inches towards
Life less than meagre.
Going down, no rest
For the unendowed
And dispossessed.
A public shroud
Conceals their fall
And the public purse
Cuts wherewithal
To make it worse.

'Mister! Mister!
Fifty pence, please!
Come oan, come oan, sir!'
Our coins appease
Sore charity,
Expense of shame
And low pity.
Oh, in whose name
But Government's
In Central Station,
Where life's laments
Offend a nation?

Low benefits
Or none at all
And that cap fits
On one and all
Who voted for
'Initiative',
That metaphor
By which they live.
The Devil's in't,
The way they quest
For self-reliant
Self-interest.

Worse than worse is
How they flatter
'Market Forces' –
Mad as a hatter!
While they grow strong
Others diminish,
From wrong to wrong
Until the finish.
Twenty per cent?
Go, tax their breath!
Jack up the rent!
'Reform', or death!

Ideologue
And Moneybags
Loathe Underdog
And The Man in Rags,
And I imagine
A similar bitch
Calls profits in
To make her rich
From this cheap kitchen,
Where a bad smell slurs
A tawdry nation
And its treasurers.

'Financial link'?
That's what you say?
That's how *you* think?
Put it this way –
I say you stink;
You tax the poor.
'Financial link'?
What is it for?
I'll tell you. Sirs,
And Madams, you
Pretend to answers
As if you knew

The questions, but
You don't. You feel
A need to 'cut'
But not to heal.
'Financial link'?
What is it *for*?
It's how you *think*.
That's what it's for.
Six million souls
In pauperdom;
A round of doles
Till Kingdom Come! . . .

For a' that, aye,
For a' that, men
Could live and die,
The angry pen
Fall from the hand
And nothing change
In this hurt land
Until that strange
Obsession dies
And begging-bowl
Free enterprise
Goes to the wall.

Women who sit
Without a bean
Articulate
The unforeseen –
From opulence
By luck or tick
To indigence
In the bus-district,
The same scrapheap
As shuttered shops,
That burst downpipe,
Those plundered skips.

'Leave them to root
In the litter-bin;
The destitute
Are guilty of sin.'
Death's dialect
Announces his
Sneered disrespect
And prejudice.
Grim children wait
While mother pays
And it grows late
For the decencies.

About The Author

DOUGLAS DUNN is a poet whose work includes *Elegies*, *Selected Poems*, and *Northlight*. He has also written a book of short stories, *Secret Villages*, and his most recent work for radio is a translation of Racine's *Andromaque*.

CHATTO
Counter*Blasts*

Also available in bookshops now:-

Forthcoming Chatto Counter*Blasts*

Plus pamphlets from Michael Holroyd, Hanif Kureishi, Michael Ignatieff and Susannah Clapp

If you want to join in the debate, and if you want to know more about **CounterBlasts**, the writers and the issues, then write to:

Random House UK Ltd, Freepost 5066, Dept MH, London WC1B 3BR